WHAT ARE COMPUTER NETWORKS AND THE INTERNET?

JENNIFER REED

IN ASSOCIATION WITH

ROSEN
EDUCATIONAL SERVICES

Published in 2018 by Britannica Educational Publishing (a trademark of Encyclopædia Britannica, Inc.) in association with The Rosen Publishing Group, Inc.
29 East 21st Street, New York, NY 10010

Distributed exclusively by Rosen Publishing.
To see additional Britannica Educational Publishing titles, go to rosenpublishing.com.

First Edition

Britannica Educational Publishing
J.E. Luebering: Executive Director, Core Editorial
Mary Rose McCudden: Editor, Britannica Student Encyclopedia

Rosen Publishing
Bernadette Davis: Editor
Nelson Sá: Art Director
Nicole Russo-Duca: Series Designer
Cindy Reiman: Photography Manager
Sherri Jackson: Photo Researcher

Library of Congress Cataloging-in-Publication Data

Names: Reed, Jennifer, 1967– author.
Title: What are computer networks and the internet? / Jennifer Reed.
Description: New York : Britannica Educational Publishing, in Association with Rosen Educational Services, 2018. | Series: Let's find out! Computer science | Includes bibliographical references and index. | Audience: Grades 1–4.
Identifiers: LCCN 2017016582| ISBN 9781680488456 (library bound : alk. paper)
| ISBN 9781680488449 (pbk. : alk. paper) | ISBN 9781538300336 (6 pack : alk. paper)
Subjects: LCSH: Computer networks—Juvenile literature. | Internet—Juvenile literature.
Classification: LCC TK5105.5 .R37226 2017 | DDC 004.6—dc23
LC record available at https://lccn.loc.gov/2017016582

Manufactured in the United States of America

CONTENTS

CONNECTING COMPUTERS

A computer is an electronic device for working with information. The information can be numbers, words, pictures, movies, or sounds. Desktops, laptops, tablets, and even smartphones are the main types of computers. Computers communicate, or talk, with other computers through networks.

A computer network is like a group of people. There are different kinds of networks that people use. These include family, school, sports, and work networks. Each person

Students can use computer networks to get homework assignments and talk to their teachers.

An Ethernet cable connects devices like computers to a local network. The cables look like telephone cords.

within a network shares and communicates information to other people in the network.

Similarly, when a computer shares information with another computer it is part of the same computer network. Cables, radio waves, and satellites can link computers to each other. These links are like glue that holds the network together.

THINK ABOUT IT

Think about all the networks you belong to. Give examples of ways you communicate with other people in your network.

THE HISTORY OF COMPUTERS

The first **digital** general purpose computer, ENIAC (Electronic Numerical Integrator and Computer) was introduced to the public in 1946. Like other early computers, its many parts took up an entire room.

ENIAC was one of the earliest digital computers.

The Programma 101 was an early version of a computer that could fit on a desk.

Computers became smaller with time. The Programma 101 was introduced in 1965. It was revolutionary because it could fit on top of a desk. It was very expensive, so it was not meant to be sold to the general public. In 1968, Hewlett-Packard introduced the HP 9100A. It was the first desktop that was a personal computer. However, the HP 9100A was sold as a calculator because people thought a computer had to be big. Since the 1960s, many companies have developed personal computers. Over the years they have become much smaller, lighter, and cheaper than the early versions. They can store and share larger amounts of information as well.

THE HISTORY OF THE INTERNET

The computer network with the most users is called the internet. It connects millions of computers worldwide. It was one of the greatest inventions of the 1900s. Today the internet helps many people communicate, work, learn, and have fun.

The internet, however, was not the first computer network. In the 1950s computer scientists began to think about ways to connect computers. At the time, most computers were large, powerful machines used by researchers at universities. The researchers

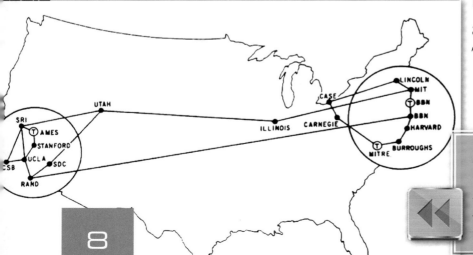

This map shows where ARPANET was being used in the early 1970s.

wanted to be able to share information. In 1969 a network called **ARPANET** connected four universities's computers. It was the first time computers could communicate and share information.

By the mid-1970s many groups of computers were connected in networks. Machines called routers were invented to connect the networks. These interconnected networks became the internet. Only people at universities and government organizations had access to the internet at first. By the 1990s, however, the internet was available to everyone.

People of all ages and from all over can access the internet on their personal devices.

THE WORLD WIDE WEB

The internet holds information and connects computers. A different technology, the World Wide Web, allows a user to access information that is on the internet. British computer scientist Sir Tim Berners-Lee is said to have invented the World Wide Web (commonly called the web) in the early 1990s. Before that, researchers had to email each other to share their results and techniques.

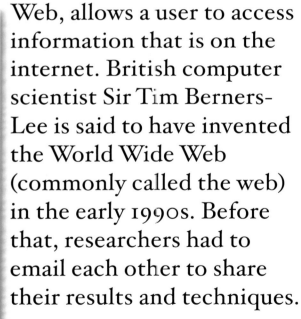

Sir Tim Berners-Lee has received many awards and honors for inventing the World Wide Web.

Google

Advanced search
Language tools

Google Search   I'm Feeling Lucky

Advertising Programs   Business Solutions   About Google

© 2011 - Privacy

Google's home page is very simple. People use Google and other search engines to look for information on the web.

The web gives users access to documents that are linked to each other through electronic connections called hyperlinks. Software called a web browser allows a user to find and view those documents. A user can search for information by using a **search engine**. There are millions of documents that anyone in the world may access because of this breakthrough in internet technology.

THE LANGUAGE OF THE WEB

Hypertext is a path, or link, to different parts of the same electronic document. The path may also lead to other documents. HyperText Transfer Protocol (HTTP) is the system of rules that explains how those links work.

This is a page of one of Encyclopedia Britannica's websites. HTML is the reason that text, images, and links appear as they do on this and other websites.

Britannica School Middle Search

Students Educators

My Britanni

CAN YOU GUESS?
Why was the Hindu temple Angkor Wat transformed into a Buddhist shrine?

READ THE ARTICLE

© Hu Xiao Fang/Shutterstock.com

MORE LIKE THIS

Explore Britannica

ARTICLES

IMAGES AND VIDEOS

BIOGRAPHIES

WORLD ATLAS

COMPARE COUNTRIES

TOUR THE U.S.A.

MY CONTENT

Can You Guess?

The Art Archive/SuperStock

David R. Frazier Photolibrary, Inc./Alamy

© Walter Holzmann/Fotolia

Why did Achilles' heel become famous?

Why did human sacrifice play such an important part in the Aztec religion?

Where is the "Roof of the World"?

THINK ABOUT IT

Why do you think computers need their own languages in order to communicate?

In order to read and write, you must know what words to use. Words come from languages like English or Spanish. In the same way, computers connecting to the World Wide Web know and understand the language called HTML. HTML stands for HyperText Markup Language. A web browser knows how to read that language and translate the information into letters and images that a user can understand.

These websites have their own URLs. URLs allow users to access content on a site.

Each website has its own internet address called a uniform resource locator, or URL. A URL is like a street address for a house, but it serves as an address for a site on the web.

DATA AND NETWORK FILE SHARING

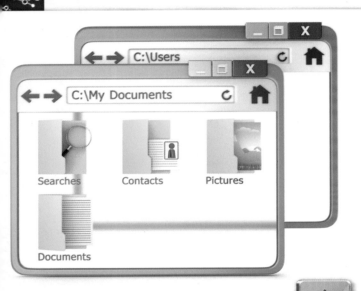

C:\Users

C:\My Documents

Searches   Contacts   Pictures

Documents

This image shows folders on a computer. Some of those folders have files sticking out of them.

Sharing data used to involve several steps. First, the data was copied to a storage device. Then, the storage device was brought from one location to another, however far that might be. Then, the computer that needed the data downloaded it to complete the transfer.

Now, people can quickly access files from the internet. This

Smartphones are a computer and cell phone in one device. You can use them to send emails, shop, or watch videos.

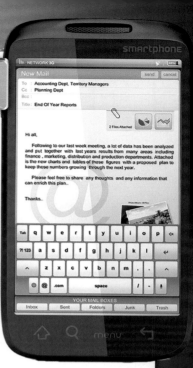

process is called network file sharing. A network connection makes network file sharing possible. That connection maintains a path that allows users to upload or copy data files. Certain software allows computers to access the place on a **server** that stores data.

Peer to peer (P2P) file sharing is another type of file sharing. It allows computers on the same network to share large files.

Attaching files to email is another option for sharing data between computers. However, email usually cannot send files with large amounts of data.

COMPUTER NETWORK HARDWARE AND SOFTWARE

Hardware for a network computer is equipment or devices you can see and touch. In order for a computer to join a network like the internet, it needs to have a network device. A network device is often a box that connects computers together so they can share files and information. They also connect computers to printers and cell phones. Some devices for connecting are hubs, switches, bridges, modems, and routers.

A router connects a computer or another device to a Wi-Fi network. Wi-Fi networks often require a password.

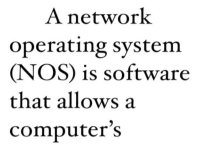

Network software and hardware work together to connect to the internet.

A network operating system (NOS) is software that allows a computer's operating system to connect to a network. Network software is a **program** found on most computers. The program tells the network hardware what to do. Network software allows computers to communicate and share files and hardware devices with each other. It also protects the network with security systems.

VOCABULARY

A **program** is a set of step-by-step instructions that tells a computer to do something with data.

WIRED CONNECTIONS

This photo shows a network switch with attached cables. It connects devices on a network.

There are two ways a computer can connect to a network. **Telecommunications systems** send information using wired or wireless connections.

A wired connection needs wires or cables. The wires or cables must be physically

A computer mouse is a peripheral device. This one is connected through the USB port of a computer.

attached to all of the most important parts of the network or the connection fails.

The wires or cables contain glass fibers or copper. Wires can transmit voice signals, computer data, and even video signals. Some devices that can receive wired signals are cable television and broadband internet service.

Devices that connect to a computer through the USB port may also be called "wired." These include the keyboard, mouse, headphones, and speakers.

WIRELESS CONNECTIONS

Wireless networks rely on different types of radio waves to send signals. Radio waves travel through the air. Devices like modems and satellites send out and receive those waves. However, some wires and cables help in the process. Wireless technology is used for other devices as well as for connecting to the internet. Those other devices include remote garage-door openers, television remote controls, and GPS receivers.

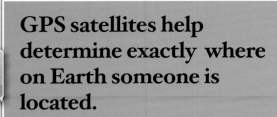

GPS satellites help determine exactly where on Earth someone is located.

THINK ABOUT IT

Sometimes when it is raining or snowing, wireless internet slows down. Why would weather affect the quality of a connection?

Wireless networks allow the user to connect to the internet anywhere and at any time. Computer networks use different types of wireless technology. Some examples of wireless technology are Wi-Fi, Bluetooth, and mobile connections.

Home networks often rely on Wi-Fi. Bluetooth uses radio waves to connect devices to a smartphone or computer. Watches, refrigerators, and many other common objects rely on wireless technology to connect to the internet.

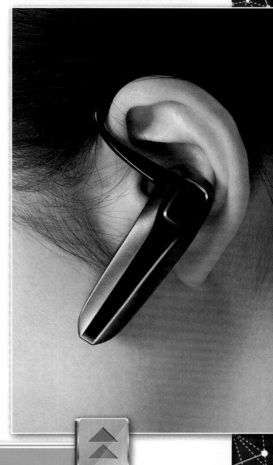

A Bluetooth headset is a device that connects to a cell phone wirelessly. It gives a user hands-free access to the phone.

LOCAL AND WIDE AREA NETWORKS

Some networks are small. They connect two or more computers to each other or to other devices. They connect devices within a building or a small group of buildings. These networks are called local area networks (LAN). Schools often choose to connect their

Computers in a school computer lab are linked to a local area network (LAN).

COMPARE AND CONTRAST

Why would someone choose to create a local area network? What about a wide area network?

computers in a LAN. Because a LAN covers a small area, fewer people may use it.

A network that connects computers over a large area is a wide area network (WAN). It can reach cities and countries all over the world. The biggest WAN is the internet. Telephone or cable lines and satellite links usually connect WANs. WANs also connect LANs. This allows computers in a small area like a school to connect to the internet.

Even computers and devices at a computer store need to be connected to the internet. Users want to know if they work well.

HOME AREA NETWORKS

A typical home network might have a computer and printer. A cell phone can also be part of the network.

A home area network (HAN) is a type of computer network that connects devices within the home to the internet. It allows these devices to share files and programs. Home networks can be either wired or wireless. With a HAN, the electrical system of

THINK ABOUT IT

Your house is alive! Would you like to live in a house that automatically raises the temperature if it gets cold, turns on lights when it is dark, or sends you recipes to make for dinner?

the home is controlled by a computer and activated by a telephone.

A home area network can control security systems, the temperature inside the house, and kitchen devices. Simple tasks like turning on or off lights can be done automatically. A washer or dryer can send a message to let you know when it is done. A refrigerator can search for recipes based on the ingredients stored inside.

This person is using a home area network to control the temperature of his house.

NETWORK PROTOCOLS

People communicate through language, both spoken and written. Computer networks have their own language. This is called a protocol. It is a set of instructions or rules. All computers must follow the same protocol in order to communicate with each other. The protocol also tells when a computer can send a

Vinton Cerf is one of the scientists who created protocols for connecting to the internet.

The "http" in this Twitter URL establishes the language necessary to access the web.

message. It limits message sending so that the receiving computer doesn't receive too much information at a time.

Protocols for connecting to the internet have been around since the 1970s, when scientists Vinton Cerf and Robert Kahn created them. Two of the main protocols, TCP and IP, stand for Transmission Control Protocol and Internet Protocol. These are the basic communication languages of the internet. The HTTP is the protocol for accessing the World Wide Web.

COMPARE AND CONTRAST

How are languages that people use to communicate similar to computer protocols? How are they different?

PROTECTING YOUR NETWORK

Bad things can happen to computers that are linked to other computers through a network. There are computer programs that hurt computers and their users. These are called malware. Malware includes computer viruses, spyware, and **worms**. These bad programs can damage files and steal personal information

> ## VOCABULARY
>
> **Worms** are malware computer programs that copy themselves and use networks to send the copies to other computers.

Malware or other problems may cause a computer to stop working altogether.

A problem has been detected and windows has
to your computer.

SYSTEM_SERVICE_EXCEPTION

If this is the first time you've seen this s
restart your computer. If this screen a
these steps:

Check to make sure any new hardware or s
If this is a new installation, ask your
for   , windows updates you might need.

    , continue, disable or remove
    . Disable BIOS memory options
    to use Safe Mode to remove or
    er, press F8 to select Advance

If p
or s

This computer repair workshop helps users learn how to fix their own computer's hardware.

without the user knowing. The programs are stored on networks, so it is important to protect your computer network.

Just as you may need to take medicine to get rid of a virus in your body, computers need a type of medicine, too. Anti-virus software helps keep viruses out or finds viruses that get in. Firewalls are another form of security. A firewall is hardware or software that keeps outside users off the network. Turning off the network if it's not being used can also help. With a secure network, exploring the World Wide Web can be both safe and fun.

GLOSSARY

browser A computer program providing access to information on a network, including websites.

communication Sending or receiving of information or a message.

data Information in numerical form for use especially in a computer.

electronic Of or related to flowing particles called electrons, or electricity.

email A system for sending messages between computers.

GPS (In full, Global Positioning System) A navigation system that uses satellites orbiting Earth to send and receive signals.

hardware A computer's physical parts.

internet A communications system that connects computers and computer networks all over the world.

Local Area Network (LAN) A computer network that links devices within a building or a small group of buildings.

malware Software that hurts or damages a computer's files or a network.

radio wave An electromagnetic wave of a frequency used for long-distance communication.

router A device that sends data from one place to another within a computer network or between computer networks.

software The programs and related information a computer uses.

technology The use of science in solving problems.

transmit To transfer from one person or place to another.

Wide Area Network (WAN) A computer network in which the computers connected may be at least half a mile apart.

FOR MORE INFORMATION

Books

Hubbard, Ben. *Using Digital Technology*. Chicago, IL: Capstone, 2017.

Lyons, Heather, Elizabeth Tweedale, and Alex Westgate. *Online Safety for Coders*. Minneapolis, MN: Lerner Publications, 2017.

Niver, Heather Moore. *Careers for Tech Girls in Computer Science*. New York, NY: Rosen Publishing, 2016.

Niver, Heather Moore. *Tim Berners-Lee: Inventor of the World Wide Web*. New York, NY: Powerkids, 2017.

Yearling, Tricia. *The World Wide Web: What It Is and How to Use It*. Berkeley Heights, NJ: Enslow Publishers, 2016.

Websites

Because of the changing nature of internet links, Rosen Publishing has developed an online list of websites related to the subject of this book. This site is updated regularly. Please use this link to access this list:

http://www.rosenlinks.com/LFO/Network

INDEX